QUEST

Y4/P5

COMPANION 2

JAMES DRIVER

Contents

UNIT 1

Discover the history of Britain through the life of a road. From Romans through Tudors and the second World War to the first motorway. What will the future hold?

UNIT 2

There are holes in the sky
Where the rain gets in,
But they're ever so small
That's why rain is thin.
Spike Milligan

Is there reason in this rhyme?

UNIT 3

● Be a local history detective.

● What is your area proud of?

● When was your house built?

Watling Street

Introduction

Before the Romans came to Britain, there were many trackways across the country, but no roads. All that changed in 43 AD, when the soldiers of the Emperor Claudius arrived.

One of the first roads the Romans built was Watling Street. It ran from the port of Rutupiae (Richborough) in the east, through the new capital city, Londinium, (London) and then north-west to the Welsh border.

AVE ATQUE VALE [HAIL AND FAREWELL]   COME HITHER

C 45 AD   1100 AD.

Watling Street was used by the Romans for almost 400 years. When the Romans finally left Britain around 410 AD, the Britons found it hard to defend themselves against attacks from overseas. People from all over Europe – Saxons, Angles, Jutes and Danes – rushed in to grab new land for themselves.

Shrewsbury

Rutupiae

●——○——● = Watling Street

By 650 AD, Britain had become a collection of small kingdoms.

In 1066, William of Normandy made himself king of England. But by now the skills of road building had been forgotten. People still used Watling Street, but it was no longer the well-cared for highway it had been when the Romans had ruled Britain.

And yet, almost 2000 years after the Romans conquered Britain, Watling Street is still in use today!

Watling Street in Roman times 43–410 AD

Who built Watling Street?

Roman roads like Watling Street were built by the Roman legions. The legions were made up of Rome's best soldiers. As well as being trained in fighting, they were taught how to make forts, walls, buildings and roads.

Caelum crebris imbribus ac nebulis foedum; asperitas frigorum abest.
("The sky is overcast. There's always rain and cloud, but at least it's not too cold."
Tacitus – Agricola 12.3)

Who chose where the road went?

The route the road was to follow was chosen by specially trained surveyors. Where possible, they chose a straight line. Straight roads meant shorter journeys.

Roman surveyors were called agrimensores.

43 AD	61 AD		c410 AD
Roman invasion of Britain	Boudicca's revolt		Romans leave Britain

0   100   200   300   400   500   600   700   800   900

How was the road built?

4. They made sure the surface of the road was curved so that the rain ran off into the drainage ditches on either side. (This curve is called a **camber**).

3. Next, they covered the second layer with a third layer of **gravel**.

5. Finally, to make the very top of the road, the soldiers used whatever materials they could find nearby. In rocky places they used stone slabs (called paving stones). In other places they used flint or chalk.

2. On top of that, they put a second layer of **smaller stones**. With every layer the road grew higher and higher.

1. First, the soldiers dug a **wide ditch** and filled the bottom with large stones.

6. Large **kerbstones** were put at the side of the road to hold in the paving stones and to make a **channel** for water to run away.

Did other Romans, apart from the soldiers, use the roads?

Many towns grew up around the Roman forts, and the countryside was full of Roman-built villas. Villas were buildings at the centre of the large farms that grew food for the towns. Having good roads meant that food could be easily transported.

Watling Street in the Middle Ages c.1066–1450

Roads in the Middle Ages

The Romans left Britain around 410 AD. The new Saxon rulers didn't like living in towns or villas. This meant they had no need to use the roads. Eventually, just like the Roman towns, the roads began to crumble and fall apart.

During the Middle Ages, travelling by road was dirty, uncomfortable and dangerous. Heavy carts often got stuck in the mud, so people who needed to transport goods, like wool or wine, used packhorses instead. Robbers hid near the roads, hoping to surprise travellers who were alone or unarmed.

The Middle Ages lasted from the 5th century until the 15th century in Western Europe.

In the 14th century, laws were passed to cut down all the trees and bushes 10 m either side of the road. This was supposed to give travellers a chance to spot any attackers. Any robbers who were caught were hanged.

Felds hath eyen, and wode have eres.
G. Chaucer, The Canterbury tales (1. 1,522), The Knight's Tale

c 410 AD
Romans leave Britain

1066
William of Normandy conquers England

0   100   200   300   400   500   600   700   800   900

Pilgrims on Watling Street

In England in the Middle Ages, many Christians made the pilgrimage to the tomb of St Thomas à Becket in Canterbury Cathedral. If they made the journey from London, they followed the route of Watling Street.

King Henry II made Thomas à Becket Archbishop of Canterbury in 1162. Later, they argued about Church matters and became enemies. In 1170, four of the King's knights killed Becket inside Canterbury Cathedral. They attacked him so fiercely with swords that they cut off the top of his head and his brains spilled out. In 1172, Pope Alexander III made Becket a saint.

What is a pilgrim?

All over the world, people with different religious faiths make special journeys to sacred places. Places are usually thought to be sacred because an important religious event took place there. Many Hindus go on pilgrimages to the River Ganges. Jews may go to the Western Wall in Jerusalem. Muslims hope to make a pilgrimage at least once in their lives to the holy city of Mecca.

Because the roads were so dangerous, pilgrims often travelled in large groups for protection. The most famous group of Canterbury pilgrims are the ones invented by the poet Geoffrey Chaucer in his collection of stories called *The Canterbury Tales*.

Original stained glass of Thomas à Becket in Canterbury Cathedral. Stained glass pictures were often used to tell stories, because many people couldn't read.

1170
Murder of Thomas à Becket

c1386
Chaucer starts to write *The Canterbury Tales*

1100   1200   1300   1400   1500   1600   1700   1800   1900   2000

Watling Street in Tudor times 1485–1603

The Tudor reign began with Henry Tudor, who became Henry VII in 1485. The Tudor monarchy ended with the death of Elizabeth I in 1603.

Actors on the road

The first theatre in England wasn't built until 1576. Before then, actors set off in search of an audience. They would load a cart with their costumes, musical instruments and enough food and drink to keep them going on the slow journey between towns. Many people thought of travelling actors as being little better than beggars.

Jog on, jog on, the foot-path way,
And merrily hent the stile-a.
A merry heart goes all the day,
Your sad tires in a mile-a.
W. Shakespeare, *The Winter's Tale*
(song at IV. iii)

When the travelling actors arrived at a town, they would try and find a place to perform. This might be the marketplace, or the yard of one of the inns along the main roads where other travellers ate, slept and rested on their long, difficult journeys. Sometimes the actors would act out their plays indoors, in the great hall of a rich man's house.

It was a hard life, and often they were driven out of town before they had a chance to perform. This was because many people thought they carried all sorts of diseases with them, or the stories they told were so exciting they would stop the young men and women in the town from doing their work!

0   100   200   300   400   500   600   700   800   900

A play called *The Widdow of Watling Streete* was published in 1607 as 'written by W.S.'. Although we don't know for sure whether it was written by William Shakespeare, we do know that the play's author was familiar with Watling Street.

William Shakespeare – the missing years

Although William Shakespeare is one of the most famous authors in the world, parts of his life are a mystery. We know he was living in Stratford-upon-Avon in 1585 and working as a playwright in London by 1592. But no one is quite sure what he did in the years in between. Some people think he may have joined one of the travelling companies of actors.

A Queen on the road

Although Queen Elizabeth I spent much of her life in London, in August and September – usually the driest months of the year – she often travelled around the country on what was called a royal progress. It took as many as 400 carts and 2000 packhorses to carry everything the Queen and her courtiers needed!

Queen Elizabeth I reigned from 1558–1603.

Dunstable, in Kent, is at the junction of Watling Street and the Icknield Way. Queen Elizabeth I visited Dunstable during her royal progresses in the 1560s and 1570s.

When the Queen went to stay with the Earl of Hertford, he had a new lake dug in the grounds of his house especially for her. He also gave her a firework display and a huge feast at which 200 servants served his guests with over 1000 glass and silver dishes!

c1386
Chaucer starts to write *The Canterbury Tales*

c1590
Shakespeare travels to London

1100 1200 1300 1400 1500 1600 1700 1800 1900 2000

Watling Street: Thomas Telford 1757–1834

By the end of the 18th century, Britain was a country full of factories. The steam engines that powered them burned tons of coal. Roads like Watling Street weren't strong enough to carry heavy loads of coal, so people began to build and use canals. Soon, barges pulled by horses were carrying coal to the factories and taking huge loads of finished goods back to the towns, or to the ports around the coast where they could be shipped abroad.

One of the greatest canal makers was Thomas Telford. Although he built canals, Telford also thought that the roads of Britain could be made as good, or even better, as they had been in Roman times.

Telford's roads

Telford remade all of Watling Street from London to Shrewsbury. But road making was expensive. To help pay for the roads, turnpikes and toll gates were set up. These were barriers or gates across the road. If you wanted to use the road, you had to pay a toll.

> Today, tolls are being introduced on some of Britain's roads, bridges and tunnels. The M6 became Britain's first toll motorway in December 2003.

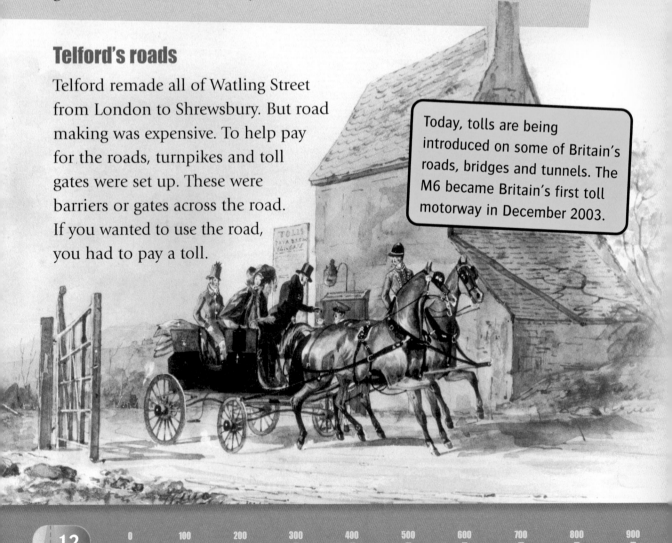

0   100   200   300   400   500   600   700   800   900

Mail coaches

On well-made roads like
Telford's new Watling Street,
mail coaches could make their
journeys much faster. Before
the invention of railways, mail
coaches were the fastest and
safest method of travel. As well
as carrying letters and parcels
quickly across the country, they also carried passengers.
The most expensive seats were inside, but you could pay less and travel outside
with the driver and the armed guard. To keep up a high speed for the whole
journey, the coachman would stop at coaching inns and change his horses.

Mail coach used on the
London to Liverpool route
in the early 1800s

The highwayman Dick Turpin
has become a legend.

Highwaymen

The speed the mail coaches went made it very
difficult for anyone to rob them, but sometimes
daring robbers would try. Armed with pistols and
mounted on fast horses, one of the gang would try
to stop the coach's horses, while another would
point his pistol at the guard to stop him from
shooting. If they did manage to stop the coach, the
highwaymen might shout, "Stand and deliver!"
This meant "Don't move! Hand over
your money!"

If a highwayman was
caught, his punishment
was usually death by
hanging!

Stand and
deliver!

c1590

Shakespeare
travels to London

c1820

Thomas Telford rebuilds the road
from London to Shrewsbury

Charles Dickens 1812–1870

Charles Dickens is one of England's most famous authors. His novels and stories are still popular today, and are often made into films, cartoons and television series.

Because Dickens was so good at describing people, places and the weather, it is easy for us to imagine what it was like to travel on roads like Watling Street in the middle of the 19th century.

Dickens became famous through a character from his first long story: Mr Pickwick from the *Pickwick Papers*.

Among many people's favourite Dickens characters are:

Ebenezer Scrooge from *A Christmas Carol*

Fagin and the **Artful Dodger** from *Oliver Twist*

Uriah Heep from *David Copperfield*

For much of the story, Mr Pickwick travels around the country with his faithful servant, Sam Weller. (Sam's father is a coachman.) The following extracts are taken from the *Pickwick Papers*.

Travelling in a coach on Watling Street

... the roads were miry, and the drizzling rain came down harder than it had done yet ... and the mud and wet splashed in at the open windows of the carriage ...

0 100 200 300 400 500 600 700 800 900

At the Saracen's Head Inn, Watling Street, Towcester

The candles were brought, the fire was stirred up, and a fresh log of wood thrown on. In ten minutes' time, a waiter was laying the cloth for dinner, the curtains were drawn, the fire was blazing brightly ...

Loading the coach in winter

Mr Pickwick and his friends are waiting in the cold on the outside of the Muggleton coach, well-wrapped up in great coats, shawls and comforters. The bags have been stowed away and Sam Weller and the guard are trying to push into the fore-boot a huge cod-fish several sizes too large for it ...

The wheels skim over the hard and frosty ground: and the horses, bursting into a canter at a smart crack of the whip, step along the road as if the load behind them were but a feather at their heels.

The coachman

The coachman, holding whip and reins in one hand, takes off his hat with the other, and resting it on his knees, pulls out his handkerchief, and wipes his forehead to show the passengers how cool he is, and what an easy thing it is to drive a four-in-hand. He adjusts his gloves, squares his elbows, cracks the whip again and on they speed.

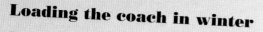

c1820 — Thomas Telford rebuilds the road from London to Shrewsbury

1836 — Charles Dickens writes the *Pickwick Papers*

Cars and trucks on Watling Street

Cars and trucks

When Charles Dickens wrote his first novel, the *Pickwick Papers*, in 1836, the fastest way to travel was by coach. By the time Charles Dickens finished his last novel, *Our Mutual Friend*, in 1865, the coaches had almost disappeared, and the most popular way to travel was by rail. But 100 years later, many of the railways had been closed. The main reason for that was the invention of the car and the truck.

> **Car journey**
> The first cars with internal combustion engine were built in the late 19th century.

> The first cars looked like horseless carriages.

By 1900, cars were looking more like cars. By the 1930s, more people owned cars due to mass production.

Since cars were built, people have always wanted to go faster and faster. In 1997, Thrust SSC (Super Sonic Car) used a jet engine to break the land speed record by travelling faster than the speed of sound.

0   100   200   300   400   500   600   700   800   900

Roads in wartime

During the Second World War (1939–1945), roads were very important in Britain. Although it was difficult for ordinary people to travel – it was very hard to buy petrol for private cars – hundreds of thousands of soldiers, sailors, airmen and their supplies were moved around the country by truck. Roads were being used for almost exactly the same reason the Romans had built them nearly 2000 years earlier!

Bletchley Park

In the war, lorry drivers followed Watling Street out of London to get to Bletchley Park. But very few of them realised just how important Bletchley Park was in winning the war. In it, hundreds of women and men worked in secret, cracking the coded messages the German leaders were sending to their forces around the world.

The first motorway

When the war ended and petrol was available again, the number of cars in Britain grew and grew. By the 1950s, there were almost 10,000,000 (10 million) cars in Britain! Traffic jams were common. To try and solve the problem, the government decided to build much bigger roads, called motorways.

What next?

But more and more people are driving cars. There are now about 24 million cars in Britain! What do you think should be done? How do you think we should travel around the country in the 21st century, 2000 years after the Romans built the first proper roads?

The M1
The first motorway, the M1, was opened in November 1959.

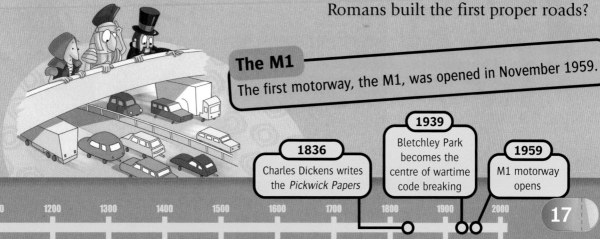

1836
Charles Dickens writes the *Pickwick Papers*

1939
Bletchley Park becomes the centre of wartime code breaking

1959
M1 motorway opens

1100 1200 1300 1400 1500 1600 1700 1800 1900 2000

Rhyme and Reason

Introduction

Many poets use ideas from science to give them inspiration for their poems. This unit is a collection of poems, together with some explanations of the science behind them.

Conductors

The Conductor

An orchestra has:
rows of violas,
lines of violins,
banks of bassoons,
mellow cellos,
tympani, tubas, trumpets,
trombones, triangles, flutes,
men in suits,
women in long evening
  dresses
clarinets and double basses,
even a harp;
but only one conductor to
  make it stop and start.

Emily Black

Look at this diagram.

In an orchestra, the conductor gives a beat to the orchestra. They play the music, and the music reaches the audience.

If you take away the conductor, the orchestra has no one to tell them what the beat is. Then the musicians play at different speeds and the music gets all mixed up. The conductor's job is to make sure the music reaches its audience correctly.

Now look at this diagram.

The battery sends electricity down the wires to the light bulb. The wires are called conductors because they carry the electricity and make sure the electricity reaches the bulb.

Conductors – you can't do without them!

If you take away or break the conductor in this electrical circuit, the electricity can't reach the light bulb, so it won't light up.

19

Habitats

Woodlice live in cool, damp, dark places. They are found in cracks in walls, rotting damp leaves and under dead tree bark. In winter, they burrow down into rotting leaves or earth to protect themselves from the cold.

I Wish I Were a Woodlouse

I wish I were a woodlouse,
In a green, mossy house,
Under a big flat stone:
I would roll into a ball
When people came to call,
And then they would leave me alone.

To be a centipede
Would be very nice indeed,
If I had fifty pairs of boots:
Or an owl in a hollow tree,
Singing "Nobody cares for me,
And I don't care two hoots."

Barn owls like to roost in old barns, hollows in trees and owl-sized nest boxes.

Robins are territorial birds so you will only find one pair in any habitat. They live in parks, gardens and woodlands. They build their nests in holes in trees, banks and walls, using twigs, moss and leaves. Sometimes they will also nest in garden sheds or other buildings.

Bright Robin Redbreast
In a kettle built his nest,
Beneath the wide, windy skies:
What does he like to eat
For his Christmas treat?
Worm pudding, and squashed flies.

John Heath-Stubbs

Did you know that a barn owl can hear a mouse's heartbeat in a dark barn?

In this Tree

In this tree
are greenflies, sawflies
and beetles burrowing,

In this tree
are ferns and mosses
and a thread of honeysuckle,

In this tree
are butterflies
feeding on sunlit leaves,

woodpeckers
searching for insects,

squirrels nesting,

In this tree
are acorns
and a notice saying:
BULL IN FIELD.

What's that noise?
What's that thundering noise
behind me?

Help!

In this tree
are all these things

and me.

June Crebbin

The Eagle

He clasps the crag with crooked hands:
Close to the sun in lonely lands,
Ringed with the azure world, he stands.
The wrinkled sea beneath him crawls;
He watches from his mountain walls,
And like a thunderbolt he falls.

Alfred, Lord Tennyson

Animals keeping their cool – and keeping warm

Bear

In wilds of old
the bear grew thin and ragged
as he lay in his cave,
dreaming of meat and honey,
of summer food and drink,
while out in the cold,
winter raged.

In zoos today,
the bear grows plump and melancholy,
the sun and warmth are there,
and food is brought
day by day,
while out in the cold,
the people stare.

Inger Hagerup and
Joan Tate

Keeping warm

Warm-blooded animals that live in really cold areas of the world – like the Arctic – may not see the sun for months. Without its warmth, they have to use other ways to keep warm.

Animals keep warm by:

- thick coats of hair or fur insulating their bodies;
- a thick layer of fat (from summer feeding) insulating their bodies;
- hibernating to save energy.

Keeping cool

Warm-blooded animals that live in really hot areas of the world – like the Sahara Desert – may have to deal with daytime temperatures as hot as 50°C. They have to find ways to keep cool.

Animals keep cool by:

- sleeping during the heat of the day;
- digging holes into the cooler ground;
- hunting at night.

mammal *noun:* any animal of which the female gives birth to live babies which are fed milk from her own body.

In hot climates, some animals have thick fur coats! In cold climates, animals also have thick fur coats!

Thick fur stops heat and cold from passing in or out. It is an insulator.

The outermost layer of hair on a camel may be up to 30°C warmer than its body temperature.

What about humans?

Humans can put more clothes on if they're cold and take them off if they're hot!

Solid and liquid

Snowflakes

And did you know
That every flake of snow
That forms so high
In the grey winter sky
And falls so far,
Is a bright six-pointed star?
Each crystal grows
A flower as perfect as a rose.
Lace could never make
The patterns of a flake.
No brooch
Of figured silver could approach
Its delicate craftsmanship. And think
Each pattern is distinct.
Of all the snowflakes floating there –
The million million in the air –
None is the same. Each star
is newly forged, as faces are,
Shaped to its own design
Like yours and mine.
And yet ... each one
Melts when its flight is done;
Holds frozen loveliness
A moment, even less;
Suspends itself in time –
And passes like a rhyme.

Clive Sansom

Making Jelly

It's my job
to take the slab of jelly
and break it up into cubes.

It's mum's job
to pour on the boiling water
to melt the cubes.

It's my job
to stir it up
until there are no lumps left.

It's her job
to put the bowl
in the fridge to help it set.

It's my job
to eat it.

Michael Rosen

Solid or liquid?

This table gives a checklist of features of solids and liquids.

Solids	Liquids
keep their shape	keep flowing until they are stopped
can be cut into different shapes	take the shape of whatever they are poured into
can be held	can't be held

Solids, liquids and gases

A substance can be a solid, liquid or a gas, depending on how hot it is. For example, liquid water becomes a solid (ice) when it is very cold and a gas (steam) when it is hot.

A solid, such as ice, has molecules that are packed tightly together.

A liquid has molecules that are close together.

A gas has molecules that move about freely.

Boiling point

The temperature at which a liquid changes to a gas is called the boiling point. (For example, when water reaches boiling point it becomes steam.)

Melting point

Heating a solid makes it melt into a liquid. Below this temperature, the liquid becomes a solid again. (For example, adding hot water to jelly cubes makes them melt into liquid jelly. Cooling it down, by putting it in the fridge, makes it become solid jelly again.)

The boiling point of water is 100°C (212°F).

The melting point of water is 0°C (32°F).

Getting about

On the Move

As a plant (a flowering one),
I turn my face towards the sun;
My roots move too: beneath the turf
They suck the water from the earth.

But if I was an elephant,
I'd walk about on pleasure bent;
I'd flex my muscles, shake the trees,
And use my trunk to eat their leaves.

Moving is done by living things
To find their food: birds flap their wings,
Fish flick their fins, and some old bloke
Strolls to the fridge and gets a coke.

Ann Winduss

Jump and Jiggle

Frogs jump
Caterpillars hump

Worms wiggle
Bugs jiggle

Rabbits hop
Horses clop

Snakes slide
Sea-gulls glide

Mice creep
Deer leap

Puppies bounce
Kittens pounce

Lions stalk –
But –
I WALK!

Evelyn Beyer

phototropic = moving towards the sun
(e.g. plant leaves and stems)
geotropic = moving towards gravity
(e.g. plant roots)

Joints

A joint is the place where two bones fit together. There are different types of joints which allow bones to move in different ways. Below are some of the different kinds of joints found in our bodies.

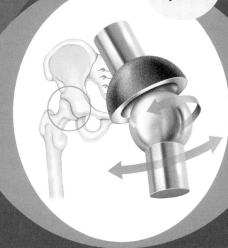

ball and socket joint

Ball and socket joint

Ball and socket joints allow for movement in almost any direction. They are found in our hips and shoulders.

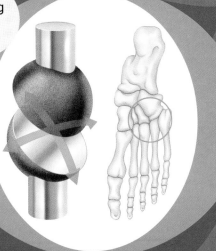

gliding joint

Gliding joints

Gliding joints contain bones that slide past each other. They let us stretch and move our hands in lots of different ways.

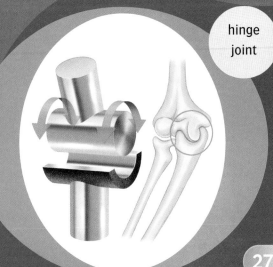

hinge joint

Hinge joint

Hinge joints allow us to bend and stretch our arms, legs, fingers and toes.

Friction

Football at Playtime

This game can't last for much longer,
And we're still only drawing: 2 – 2,
My trainers are sticking their tongues out
And it feels like their soles have worn
  through.

At least I've got something to grip with –
Joe's playing in goal in his shoes!
He's slipping about like a penguin –
It's him who I'll blame if we lose.

Sarah-Jane Stephens

Waiting at the Window

These are my two drops of rain
Waiting on the window-pane.

I am waiting here to see
Which the winning one will be.

Both of them have different names.
One is John and one is James.

All the best and all the worst
Comes from which of them is first.

James had just begun to ooze.
He's the one I want to lose.

John is waiting to begin.
He's the one I want to win.

James is going slowly on.
Something sort of sticks to John.

John is moving off at last.
James is going pretty fast.

John is rushing down the pane.
James is going slow again.

James has met a sort of smear.
John is getting very near.

Is he going fast enough?
(James has found a piece of fluff.)

John has hurried quickly by.
(James was talking to a fly.)

John is there, and John has won!
Look! I told you! Here's the sun!

A. A. Milne

Facts about friction

Q: What is friction?

A: Friction happens when two surfaces rub against each other.

When two **rough** surfaces rub against each other, the friction they produce slows everything down.

When two **smooth** surfaces rub against each other, there is hardly any friction, so everything speeds up!

For different kinds of sports you need different amounts of friction. You wouldn't want to be sliding about when you were climbing a steep rock face, but you would need to glide smoothly if you were an ice skater.

Which shoes would you choose for:
- skating;
- climbing;
- running;
- sliding?

29

Time travel

Talking Time-Travel Blues

Strap me in your time machine
let the motors whirr
switch controls to speed of light
make my senses blur.

Batten down the airlocks
make all the hatches fast
blast me through the chronosphere
ferry me through the past.

Take me back three thousand years
roll back the centuries
I want to see what Earth was like
2000th year AD.

Show me what the world was like
before we burnt the trees
killed off all the animals
and dried up all the seas.

Let me see a clear blue sky
windswept clouds and rain.
I'd love to see the wild Pacific,
hear people laugh again.

I'd like to know how coal was used
and just what oil was for.
Whatever happened to rich
 gold seams
And other precious ore?

Living in these sterile domes
is simply not for me.
I can't stand food in capsule form.
I need a world that's free.

So strap me to your time machine
let the engine whine
turn the dials to speed of light
I'm Earth bound – just in time.

Adrian Rumble

Is time travel possible?

Lots of people would love to travel through time. Some would like to go back into the past and discover what really happened in history. (Where did pirates bury their treasure? What really happened to the dinosaurs?)

Others would prefer to go forward in time and discover what life will be like in the future. (Will we live on other planets? What will happen when we run out of oil? Will teachers be replaced by computers?)

But, the more scientists think about time travel, the more problems they find.

Squashed up time

Some people think the answer to time travel can be found in black holes. A black hole is what's left after a giant star dies. After a huge explosion, the star collapses and pulls all the space around it into one tiny spot – like a vacuum cleaner sucking up a sheet.

According to one of the world's most famous scientists – Albert Einstein (1879–1955) – if you change the shape of space by crumpling it up, you change the shape of time too. So, if a black hole is full of crumpled up space, perhaps it's full of crumpled up time as well, and a spaceship travelling fast enough into one of these black holes might find a way to get to where it started before it left!

Q: But if time travel is possible, why haven't we had any visitors from the future?

Local History Detective

Introduction

Have you ever wondered what happened in days long ago in the place where you live? What did your road look like 100 years ago? What jobs did people do? To discover the history of where you live – and to make some predictions about the future – you can become a history detective. Luckily, there are clues everywhere – you just have to know where to look!

Newmarket

History detective in Newmarket

Newmarket is a small town on the Suffolk/Cambridgeshire border in East Anglia. It is known as the 'Headquarters of Racing' in Britain. There are over 60,000 racehorses in training in Newmarket. The old market was in nearby Exning. According to local legend Exning was smitten by plague in the 14th century, so people wouldn't go there any more, and a New Market was established 5 km away. Today, you can find many clues to Newmarket's past.

Houses

There are examples of Georgian houses in Newmarket's High Street. You can see the sash windows and small panes of glass that are typically Georgian. These buildings used to be houses for rich people. Today, they are used mainly as offices.

In what is now Jane's dressmakers in the High Street, there is a basement that was used as a cock-fighting pit. Now, customers from the dress shop drink coffee there!

Natural history

Clues to history aren't always buildings or monuments. History detectives can find out about where they live by looking at natural things like rivers, forests and open spaces.

The Devil's Dyke runs alongside Newmarket's racecourses. The Dyke (a deep ditch) was built in Anglo-Saxon times to stop romanised invaders from the west of England invading the kingdoms of the Anglo-Saxons in East Anglia.

Public art

From the earliest days, people have made sculptures, pictures and monuments and displayed them where they live. People make public art for many reasons:

- as reminders of people, animals or events;
- to give the name of a place and show something about its history;
- to remember a special occasion or festival.

Public art can be permanent or temporary, but it always tells us something about the place in which it stands, and the people who put it there.

Monuments to events

This memorial fountain in Southampton commemorates the sinking of the great ship, the *Titanic*, on 15 April 1912. The ship sailed from Southampton and many local people would have been on board.

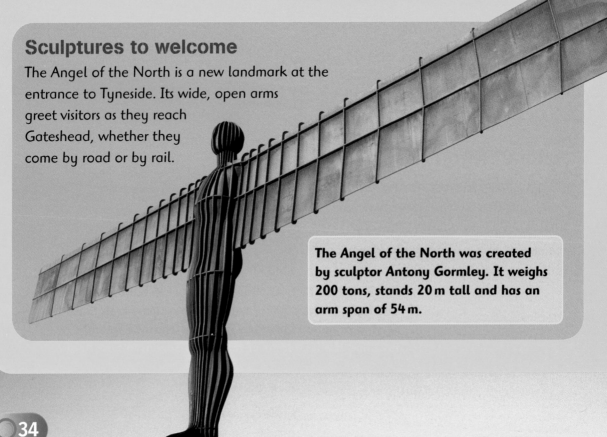

Sculptures to welcome

The Angel of the North is a new landmark at the entrance to Tyneside. Its wide, open arms greet visitors as they reach Gateshead, whether they come by road or by rail.

The Angel of the North was created by sculptor Antony Gormley. It weighs 200 tons, stands 20 m tall and has an arm span of 54 m.

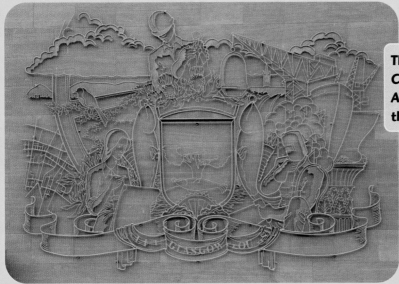

This sculpture is the Glasgow Coat of Arms, designed by Andrew Scott in 1996. It shows things linked with Glasgow.

War memorials

War memorials list the people from the community who were killed in war.

Unexplained art

We don't always know what public art means. No one knows why this white horse was created. It might have been to celebrate winning a battle. It may have been the badge of the tribe who lived here. It was made by cutting lines of the green turf away from the hillside, leaving the white chalk soil beneath. It is Britain's most famous and oldest hill figure at 2000–3000 years old.

White Horse at Uffington, Oxfordshire

What public art can you find in your local community? What does it tell you about where you live?

It's all in the name

Street names

The names given to the streets in your local area can often tell you a great deal about what happened there in the past.

Look at what one history detective discovered about some of the street names in Dover.

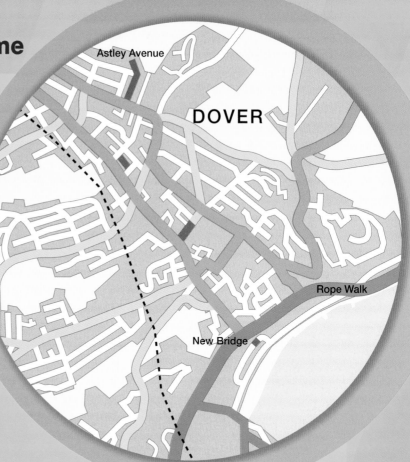

Astley Avenue

DOVER

Rope Walk

New Bridge

New Bridge

Today, there is no sign of any bridge, old or new! The river now runs out of sight under all the new buildings that have been put up since 1840.

Astley Avenue

This avenue was named after Dr Edward F. Astley, who was mayor of Dover between 1858 and 1859. He paid for the building of a hospital in the town and gave the town hall a brand new organ.

Rope Walk

This road is in the area where long ropes were made for the sailing ships that used Dover as a harbour. A long straight area was needed, as the large ropes were made by twisting together lengths of smaller rope.

Place names

Over the last 2000 years, many different settlers and invaders have lived and landed in the British Isles – Celts, Romans, Saxons, Vikings and Normans among them.

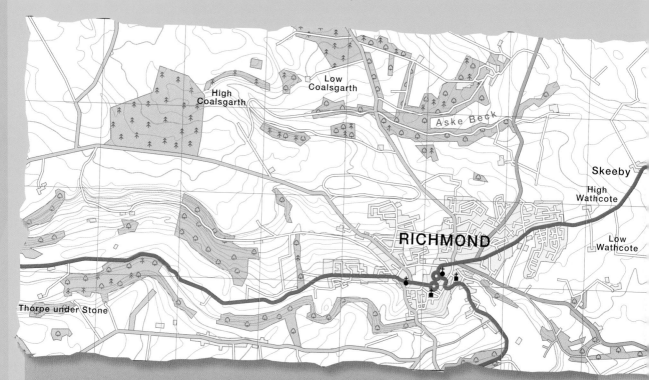

A good way for history detectives to discover who settled in their area is to look at the clues in the place names. The best place to start is often at the end of the word.

This map is of a part of North Yorkshire.

Can you find places with these words in them?

mond is a Norman word meaning hill

by is a Viking suffix meaning farm or village

beck is a Viking name meaning stream

cote is a Saxon word meaning cottage

garth is a Viking word meaning a place guarded by a wall

thorp is a Viking word meaning farm or village

It looks like this area was once a place where there were lots of Viking settlers.

Does your house tell a story?

The buildings around you can tell you a lot about local resources, traditions and the people who built them.

Doors

The most important outside feature of a building is the front door. As well as being a gangway for people (and animals) and providing security, it lets in light when open or glazed, and keeps the weather out.

Half-doors were often used because they let light and fresh air in while keeping the chickens and other animals out.

The height of a door indicates the height people were in the times when it was built. As people have become taller, doors have had to be made taller too.

Windows

The word window comes from 'wind-hole' – an opening in the wall or roof to let in air for fire. To stop birds or intruders coming in, the wind-hole was often criss-crossed with reeds in a diamond pattern.

Although the Romans made glass at Glastonbury in England and had perfected methods of rolling out large slabs of glass to make windows, these techniques were not carried on after they left.

After the Romans left England, any glass Britain needed was imported. It was expensive and small, so that it didn't break when travelling. Tudor (16th century) windows like this one used decorative patterns to disguise the fact that the pieces of glass were very small.

In the 17th century, the vertical sliding sash window was introduced from Holland. Only the bottom sash opened; the top one was fixed. Not until Georgian times did both sashes move.

43–409 AD
Roman invasion of Britain

410–1065 AD
Invaders

0   100   200   300   400   500   600   700   800   900

During the late 1800s, the Victorians often replaced the top panels of their front doors with coloured glass. As well as making the doors more attractive, the glass let in more light than a solid door. Because it was coloured, people still couldn't see inside.

Some doors have porches built around them. As well as giving some protection from the weather, porches are used to show off the owner's wealth and style.

Nowadays, many old barns and warehouses have been converted into houses. They often have doors which are wider than most house doors because they were built for animals.

This window is classic Georgian style. The panes are still small because large pieces of glass were difficult and expensive to manufacture and to transport to the house.

The Victorians' houses were often very decorated, both inside and out. Bay windows, as well as coloured glass, were a feature. During Victorian times, sheet glass, which let in more light, became more easily available.

Between 1696 and 1851, house owners had to pay taxes based on the number of windows in their house. As a result, many windows were blocked up.

1066–1215	1216–1347	1348–1484	1485–1603	1603–1714	1714–1837	1837–1901
Normans	The Middle Ages	Late Medieval	Tudors	Stuarts	Georgians	Victorians

1100   1200   1300   1400   1500   1600   1700   1800   1900   2000

Walls

Stone houses are much more difficult to build than timber ones, but the advantage is that they are fireproof. Early stone houses weren't built with cement and mortar, so the walls had to be made very thick to make them stand up. Throughout history, the cheapest stone has always been the one that is available locally. Are any of these your local stone?

Cotswold stone in Gloucestershire

Granite in Ireland

Bricks

Bricks weren't used for building ordinary houses until the 15th century. Today, they are the most common building material in many areas. The colour of a brick depends on the type of earth it has been made from. It can also tell you when the house was built. Which one is your house made from?

The word brick comes from the French 'brique'.

Where there is a lot of iron, the bricks are red (e.g. Lancashire) or, when baked in very hot temperatures, blue (e.g. Staffordshire).

Black bricks from South Wales, Surrey and Berkshire contain manganese.

43–409 AD
Roman invasion of Britain

410–1065 AD
Invaders

0   100   200   300   400   500   600   700   800   900

Dry slate-walled houses in Wales

East Anglian knapped (broken) flint

Sandstone in Yorkshire and Scotland

Brandon, in Suffolk, East Anglia, became known as the flint-knapping centre of Europe. Flints from Brandon were exported to Europe for use as gun flints.

Brown bricks (e.g. Humberside) contain lots of lime but not much iron.

Yellow bricks from the Thames valley contain sulphur and chalk.

White and grey bricks (e.g. Sussex, East Anglia, Hampshire, Oxfordshire and Berkshire) contain lime but no iron.

In the mid-18th century, stone-like colours (white, grey, yellow) were preferred.

1066–1215	1216–1347	1348–1484	1485–1603	1603–1714	1714–1837	1837–1901
Normans	The Middle Ages	Late Medieval	Tudors	Stuarts	Georgians	Victorians

1100　　1200　　1300　　1400　　1500　　1600　　1700　　1800　　1900　　2000

Buildings in industry

In every village, town and city, there are clues about what jobs people used to do and what their working lives were like.

Industrial town

Since the Industrial Revolution, people have moved from the countryside into towns and cities to look for work. Industrial buildings were often large and plain; they had to be large to fit in lots of machinery, materials and people, and they were plain and undecorated because it wasn't worth spending money on what they looked like.

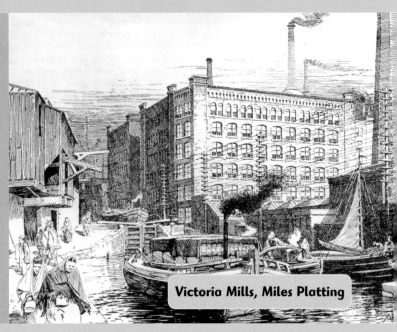

Victoria Mills, Miles Platting

Workers' homes

As well as factories, other buildings can give clues to your area's industrial past. All the workers who worked in the factories needed somewhere to live. Most of them would have lived close to the factories. The factory workers' houses were small, dark and cold. There were often up to ten people sharing one room and people went to bed in shifts because there weren't enough beds for everyone.

Workers' houses, Glasgow, 1860s

After the Second World War, people found that it was cheaper to buy textiles and cotton from other countries. Today, most of the factories and mills are not working. Many of them have fallen into ruin, but others are now being used for other things.

Tate Modern art gallery

In 1981, the Bankside Power Station in London was closed. In 1995, the Tate art gallery needed more space to display its modern art and the old power station was just the right size.

The power station was built from more than 4.2 million bricks. The height of the central chimney was limited to 99m in order to be lower than the dome of nearby St Paul's Cathedral.

The empty Turbine Hall in the Tate Modern

It took a large team of men and machines five years to convert the power station to an art gallery. The art is displayed in the old Boiler House and Turbine Hall, as well as other parts of the power station, so visitors can get a good idea of what working inside the power station may have been like.

20th-century architecture

During the 20th century, many different materials were developed, some of which could be used for building houses. New technology meant that scientists and engineers could experiment in a way that was never possible before.

Quick and easy prefabricated buildings

Quick and easy buildings

During the two World Wars (1914–1918 and 1939–1945), new buildings were needed for houses, offices and factories because many people were moving to different places to train for war or to do war jobs. Quick and easy buildings were built. Although these buildings were meant to be temporary, some of them are still standing today.

prefabricated *adjective:* made in sections ready to be assembled on site.

The space race

Many designers and architects in the 20th century have been influenced by books, television programmes and films about space.

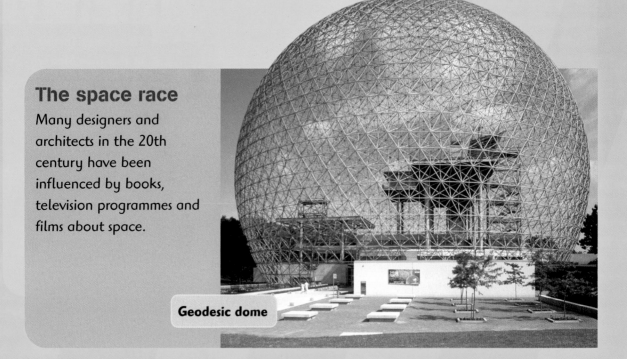

Geodesic dome

	1903 First flight by the Wright brothers	1914–1918 First World War	1922 First radio broadcast by the BBC	1936 First television transmission	1939–1945 Second World War
1900	1910	1920	1930	1940	1950

Eco-friendly buildings

Increasingly during the 20th century, people have been aware of the environmental effects of how they live and what it means for the future of the Earth. Environmentally friendly – or eco-friendly – materials and ways of building began to be developed and introduced.

This American house is being built with straw bales in the walls.

Building with straw bales

Some people build with straw bales because it's cheap (because bales are easily available), easy and quick. Many owners can build their houses themselves, in a matter of days or weeks. Straw bale buildings also have good insulating properties, which makes them economical to keep warm.

Some houses are now built with 'green' roofs – roofs made of sedum (a plant) and moss mats – which provide good insulation, are cheap and benefit the environment.

What next?

Where do you think you'll be living in the 21st century?

1953
Coronation of
Elizabeth II
1960

1969
First man walked
on the moon
1970

1982
Falklands War
1980

1991
First Gulf War
1990

45

Moon Stones

by Douglas Hill

1 Children of the dome

Dav and his friend Jeni were reading book-pods in the games room – ignoring the teenagers playing four-way robo-pool – when the door crashed open.

Caryn, one of the younger scientists, burst in.

"Come and see what we've found!" she cried, and whirled away.

The teenagers galloped after her, with Dav and Jeni close behind. None of them had any idea what they might see, but they knew it was likely to be amazing.

Most things were, for people living inside a dome on a frozen, dangerous place millions of miles from Earth.

The frozen, dangerous place was Europa, one of the moons of the planet Jupiter. Earth had sent a team of scientists to study Europa, living inside a protective dome. And some had brought their families – so Dav was there with his mother, one of the leading scientists. Dav was nearly eleven, the youngest of the dome's six children – thin, dark-haired, serious-minded.

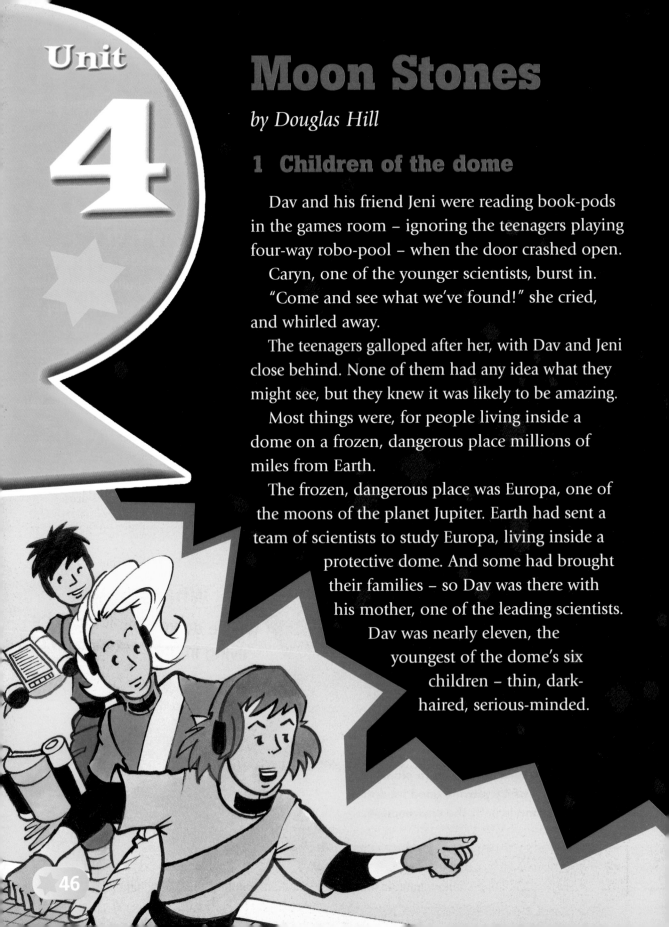

He, too, planned to be a space scientist when he grew up.

Most of all, he wanted to meet an alien.

So he was quivering with curiosity as they followed Caryn out of the building. It was where everyone lived and worked – a flat square building, made of super-tough metal. The high, broad dome around it was made of special plastic, as tough as the super-metal but perfectly clear.

So nothing blocked the view of the sky – almost filled by the unbelievably huge, many-coloured mass of Jupiter. And there was also a clear view of the ice that covered Europa, gleaming in Jupiter's light. The dome had been placed on one of the biggest, flattest ice fields – rough and bumpy in places, but with no spiky crests or deep clefts.

Caryn led the children to the front of the dome, where everyone had gathered to look at the discovery. But it was still far away, near the long rugged ridge that marked the edge of their ice field.

"I can't make out what it is," complained Alind, the oldest of the teenage boys.

"It's huge blocks of ice," Caryn said. "Piled up high – and really square and even, like giant ice cubes …!"

"Not only that," said a bulky man named Wolt, another of the leaders, standing beside Dav's mother.

"The scanners show some sort of object inside each block of ice," his mother said. "Have a look."

She held out a hand-scanner. Alind took it, peered, said "Wow!", then passed it on. When it was Dav's turn, he was amazed at the size of the heaped-up blocks of ice, and how smooth and clear they were. But he was most amazed by the strange dark shapes inside them.

"They could've been put there by aliens!" he breathed.

Everyone laughed at him, as usual. "It's probably a natural formation," Wolt said. "We'll learn more when we get there."

But no one would have to make a special trip to look at the ice blocks. The dome itself would get there.

JUPITER

- fifth planet from the Sun (Earth is third)
- biggest planet in our solar system; bigger than all the other planets put together
- not solid, but made of liquids and gases
- covered in thick cloud layers like stripes or 'belts', in many colours – dusky-red, yellow, brown, blue-grey
- orbited by four large moons and dozens of smaller ones
- three of Jupiter's four large moons (Callisto, Ganymede and Io) are bigger than our moon; the fourth, Europa, is slightly smaller

Slowly, the dome was *moving* across the ice field, and floating half a metre above the ice on a cushion of energy. But it stopped, settling, while machines beneath it studied the ice, drilling down for samples. And other machines looked even deeper, scanning the ocean that lay below Europa's frozen surface.

Dav usually liked watching the dome's front edge drifting majestically forward. But over the next day or two, he wished impatiently that it would hurry up. "I still think those ice blocks look like they were *put* there," he grumbled to Jeni.

Jeni smiled. She was a slim, fair-haired, quiet girl, a year older than Dav. And though she didn't laugh or tease him when he went on about aliens, as the others did, he often made her smile.

"Just wait and see," she said soothingly.

Celestial bodies

STAR: a giant ball of fiery gases, pouring out heat and light. Our Sun is a young, middle-sized star.

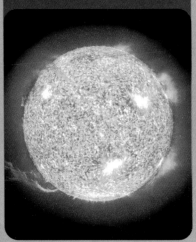

MOON: an even smaller ball in orbit around a planet, like Earth's moon. Other planets, like Mercury, have no moons; some, like Jupiter, have lots.

PLANET: a smaller ball that can be solid like Earth, or liquid, or gas, travelling in 'orbit' around a star. Several planets around a star make a 'solar system'.

49

EUROPA

- Europa is not only Jupiter's fourth largest moon, but the second closest to it.
- Europa is only 700,000 km away from Earth.
- Its surface is covered in ice – several kilometres thick in places.
- The ice has fairly smooth patches but can be quite rough, with a network of long criss-crossed ridges, probably where the ice once cracked, then froze over again.

So more days passed, until at last they were close enough to see the ice blocks clearly without hand-scanners. That evening, when everyone was gathered together, the leaders announced what would happen.

"We'll stop the dome beside the ice blocks," Wolt said. "Then we'll melt them, and bring in the things inside them."

"What do you think they are?" Alind asked.

"They're a strange kind of stone," Dav's mother said. "And every one is different. But that's about all the scanners can tell us."

"Except they're interesting shapes, all curves and coils," said a balding man named Billon. "And smooth, almost polished ..."

"Hey, Davvie!" Alind said, grinning at Dav. "Maybe they're *statues*, made by aliens!"

Everyone laughed, as always, and even Jeni and Dav's mother smiled, as Dav glowered.

"Any life on Europa is likely to be tiny ocean creatures, not alien sculptors," Wolt chuckled. "Let's keep a lid on the wild ideas, till we can study those things."

And that was the night when the children of the dome had the dreams.

2 A ghostly voice

"It was spooky!" Dav told his mother next morning. "I dreamed I was *inside* one of those blocks of ice! But I could breathe, and I was warm ... And this voice was whispering ..."

"Scary," his mother murmured. "What was it saying?"

"That was really scary," Dav said. "It said if we melt the blocks of ice, something *terrible* will happen!"

His mother smiled. "That's quite a dream. But don't worry. We'll be careful – as we always are, with things we find in space."

Dav wanted to say that the dream didn't mean "be careful". It meant "keep off". But he knew his mother wasn't taking his dream seriously. Nor would any of the other grown-ups.

It was even scarier when Dav learned that all the children had had vague, weird dreams about the ice blocks. But none of them had dreamed that they were inside the ice, nor had they heard a spooky voice. And certainly no one else was worried.

Even Jeni – the only other person Dav told about *his* dream – wasn't bothered. "It was just a dream, Dav," she said. "It doesn't *mean* anything."

But Dav stubbornly believed that it did.

He began going to the front of the dome every day, as it crept closer to the frozen heap. Staring out at it, he felt a churning mixture of feelings – curiosity about the stones in the ice blocks; anxiety about the warning in his dream.

But he was tired of being laughed at, so he said nothing. Not until the day when the dome was even closer to the ice blocks, and Dav's anxiety turned to terror.

He was standing near the dome's doorway, which was protected by a glowing power-screen. As usual, he was staring at the ice blocks, and the shapes inside them. Won't everybody be surprised, he thought, if they really *are* statues ...

With that thought, something else came into his mind as well. The ghostly voice from his dream – repeating its warning.

Do not harm the blocks of ice, or death will follow.

Fearfully, Dav spun round, but saw only Jeni, coming towards him – and Alind, with the other teenagers, ambling past nearby.

"Jeni!" Dav called urgently. "Did you hear something? Sort of *whispering?*"

As she shook her head, wide-eyed, Alind whooped with laughter. "You going space-crazy, Davvie?" he said. "Hearing voices?"

Dav turned stiffly away. He *had* heard the voice – he knew he had. But it was clear that no one would believe him. And that made him furious – and afraid.

If the voice was real, then so was the warning. Which meant that the dome could be facing some unknown, terrifying danger.

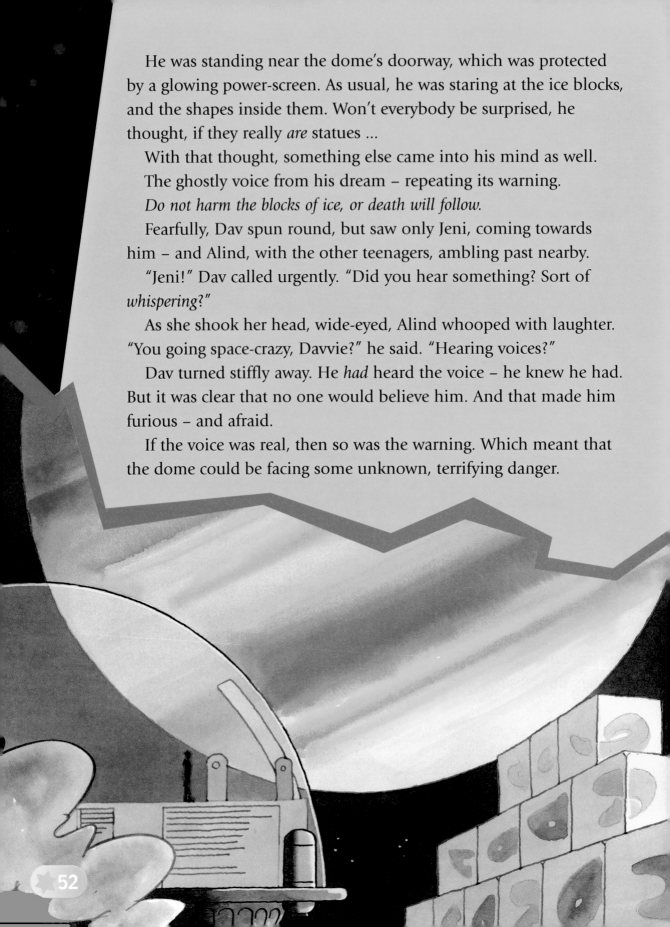

3 Invisible force

That evening, when they were all gathered together again, Wolt announced that the dome would be stopped in the morning, beside the ice blocks.

"So stay inside the building, everyone," Dav's mother said. "We'll be opening the doorway for the robots."

Everyone nodded. It was sensible to send work-robots out rather than going out themselves, in clumsy spacesuits, taking risks.

"The robots will melt the ice blocks with lasers," Billon added, "then haul in those stone shapes."

Dav desperately wanted to tell them to wait, not to melt the ice ... but he knew they wouldn't listen.

That night he lay awake, fearfully remembering the voice's warning. And he was also calling – silently, in his mind – to whatever it was that had spoken to him.

Please, he called. *Please speak to Wolt and my mum. Tell* them *not to melt the ice blocks. They won't listen to me.*

Then he went very still, barely breathing, as the voice replied. But not with another warning.

It simply said – *You must come.*

With a gasp, he found that he was getting up and leaving his room, without meaning to. As if he was a puppet, being controlled by an invisible force.

He struggled against it, but still he kept moving – out of the building, towards the dome's doorway with its power-screen.

And *through* it.

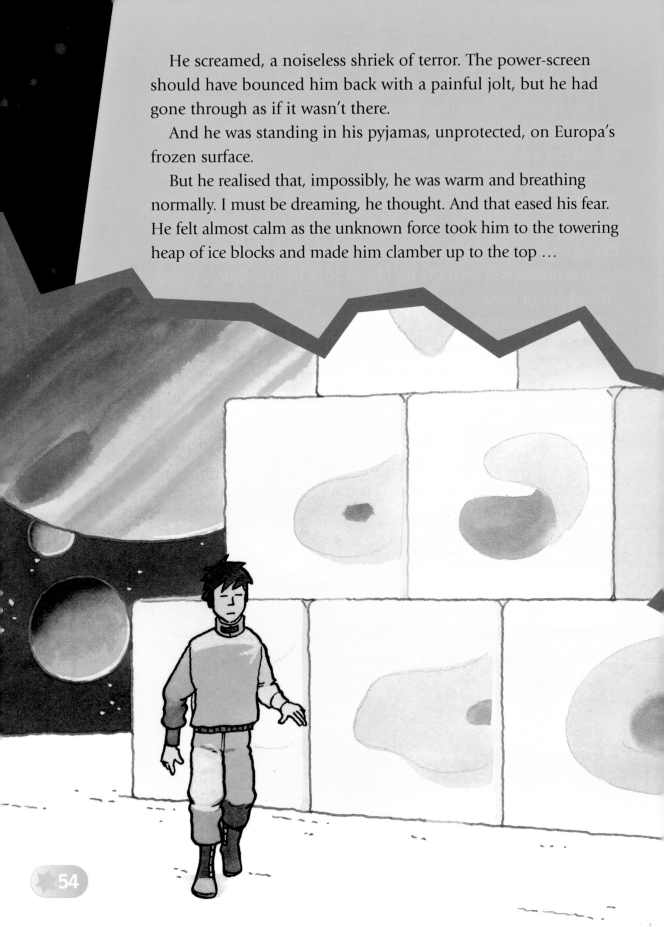

He screamed, a noiseless shriek of terror. The power-screen should have bounced him back with a painful jolt, but he had gone through as if it wasn't there.

And he was standing in his pyjamas, unprotected, on Europa's frozen surface.

But he realised that, impossibly, he was warm and breathing normally. I must be dreaming, he thought. And that eased his fear. He felt almost calm as the unknown force took him to the towering heap of ice blocks and made him clamber up to the top …

… Where ice began forming around him.

A moment later, he was standing inside a large clear ice block of his own. Yet he was still warm, still breathing. Like that other dream, he thought.

The eerie voice whispered in his mind. *Not a dream. You are truly here. To keep your people away from us.*

"What do you mean?" Dav gasped. "Who are you?"

And the voice explained.

It said that it was the combined voice of many alien beings – who were the stony shapes held within the blocks of ice.

They were a family group from a race of aliens living in Europa's ocean. At some point in their lives, each family group had to make their way up, through open cracks in the ice, onto the surface. There – with their skin hardened to stone – they gathered ice around themselves to form a heap of ice-blocks, and went to sleep.

"Sleep?" Dav repeated, startled. "Sort of like animals on Earth that hibernate in winter?"

Yes, the voice said. *But our sleep lasts many of your years …*

During that sleep, the voice went on, their minds stayed active. Linked together, they pondered deep alien problems and developed strange powers.

But though their powers let them touch other minds, they could not speak to those who would not listen. So in the end they spoke only to Dav. And though they were strong enough to control him, they could not control the adults. Nor could they stop the dome.

So they had wrapped Dav in a bubble of warm air, and brought him out onto the ice blocks to keep the humans from melting them.

"But they'll melt them to get me out!" Dav cried.

If they do, said the voice, *death will follow.*

4 Understanding

"You mean you'll kill them?" Dav whispered.

The voice seemed stronger, sterner, as if deeply upset. *We do not kill*, it said. *You have not understood ... If our ice blocks are melted before we are ready to emerge, We will die!*

Dav gulped. "I ... I'm sorry. I didn't know ... You must take me back inside, so I can tell them!"

Tell them from here, the voice said.

Dav realised then that someone in the dome had spotted him inside his ice block on top of the pile. Everyone was rushing to the front of the dome, staring out at him – including his mother, looking horrified.

Tell them, the voice repeated. *They will hear.*

So, though he had no idea how anyone in the dome could hear, Dav obeyed.

Shakily, he began to repeat what the voice had said about the aliens and their strange powers.

As he spoke, he was staring through the clear ice at the people in the dome. And he saw Jeni – at the front of the crowd – suddenly jump, looking scared. Then she turned and began talking urgently to the others.

The aliens are sending my words into her mind, Dav guessed. And she's telling everyone. At least they'll believe me now, he thought. Since I'm standing here buried in ice ...

When he (and Jeni) finished speaking, Dav saw his mother, with tears in her eyes, quickly say something to the other leaders, who all nodded. Then he heard the whispery alien voice again.

Your leaders have understood, it said. *They will not harm us.*

And Dav saw the dome begin to move backwards, away from the ice blocks.

At once, the ice vanished from around Dav. He found himself climbing down from the heap, controlled again by the alien power – then walking safely back through the dome's doorway. Into the arms of his mother, as everyone – even the teenagers – clustered around admiringly.

"Dav, you're a hero!" Jeni breathed.

"Right!" Caryn agreed, grinning. "The first human ever to speak with an alien!"

Dav was grinning too, as his mother hugged him tight. But then the alien voice drifted into his mind again.

We are grateful to you, young one, it said. *And to your people. Tell them that our sleep will end in 15 of your years. If your people are here when we emerge, we will greet them then.*

Someone will be here, Dav promised silently. *I'll be here.* Nothing in the world – in the *universe* – could keep me away.

VISITORS FROM EARTH

● Since the 1970s, scientists have sent space probes to the outer planets, including Jupiter.

● In 1995, the space probe *Galileo* became the first to get close to Jupiter by going into orbit around it. While studying Jupiter, *Galileo* sent a smaller probe to Europa, where it looked below the surface ...

Galileo was the first spacecraft to orbit Jupiter.

What Galileo saw

● *Galileo's* close look at Europa found that the ice crust covers a large ocean of slushy ice water. At its centre, Europa is probably very hot – like Earth's core. The ocean bed might also have currents of warmer water. These might explain the criss-crossed signs of cracks in the ice.

In September 2003, *Galileo* ended its mission by plunging into Jupiter's atmosphere, where it burned up and broke into tiny pieces. *Galileo* was running low on fuel and might have crashed into Europa if it had been allowed to keep orbiting.

Cinderella Stories

By Elaine Canham

Why are we still telling tales?

People all over the world have always told stories. Before television or books were invented, before pen and ink, before printing presses, story-tellers travelled from community to community telling the tales they had gathered.

From the beginning of man's time on Earth, stories have provided people with entertainment and information. Cavemen boasted to each other about the animals they had killed, Viking warriors told stories about their battles; even the Bible is made up of stories that have been gathered about God.

As the years went by and communities grew and changed, so did the stories. Many people worked on the land for the local lord, who lived in a big house or castle. Not many people could read and there was no electricity or television. So, when the sun went down, families got together and told stories, making them up around what they knew of these rich and powerful men and their wives and servants. Sometimes the lords were bullies, and characters like the rich and cruel man Bluebeard, who killed his wives, were born. Sometimes they were ugly, and tales like *Beauty and the Beast* were told.

Heroine who is a girl in a million

The story of Cinderella is thought to have first been told in China, about 1000 years ago. But there are versions all around the world. There are at least 500 versions in Europe.

The story we all know in Britain comes from France. More than 300 years ago, a lawyer called Charles Perrault wrote down the tale he heard and called it *Cendrillon*. The heroine became known as Cinderella in Britain, but in Eastern Europe she is called Marouckla. In China she is Yeh-Shen; in West Africa, Chinye; and in the Philippines, Abadeh.

All the stories have what is called a universal theme – which means they all tell the same story in different ways – of how a young girl, or sometimes a boy, overcomes hardship and cruelty to find true happiness.

Every country in the world seems to have a Cinderella story. Not all of the heroines are called Cinderella. Can you match the countries on the map with their stories?

HEROINE	COUNTRY / REGION
Abadeh	Philippines
Angkat	Cambodia
Cap o'Rushes	Scotland
Catskinella	USA (African American)
Chinye	West Africa
Damura	the Spice Islands
Kleting Kleting	Indonesia
Konjwi	Korea
Marouckla	Eastern Europe
Rhodopis	ancient Egypt
Settareh	Iran
Tam	Vietnam
Cinderella	England
Yeh-Shen	China

Cinders Gets her Prince
A tale from France

This is a version of the Cinderella story that Charles Perrault made famous.

Once upon a time, there was a rich man who had a beautiful daughter. When his wife died he married again; to a woman who already had two daughters of her own. This woman was cruel and made her new stepdaughter wear rags and work in the kitchen, while she lavished money and attention on her own daughters. The girl was nicknamed Cinderella because she kept warm at night by sleeping in the ashes of the fireplace.

One day, Cinderella's stepmother and her nasty stepsisters were invited to a ball at the palace. Cinderella was asked too, but her stepmother refused to let her go. Instead, Cinderella had to get her sisters ready, and then was left at home. She was weeping by the fireplace when her fairy godmother appeared and told her not to fret.

The fairy godmother turned a pumpkin into a gold coach, and Cinders' rags into a beautiful dress. The old shoes Cinderella was wearing became a pair of glass slippers.

So Cinders went to the ball and the prince fell in love as soon as he saw her. At midnight, Cinders remembered she had only seconds before the magic disappeared, and she ran from the palace, leaving one of her shoes behind. The next day, the prince vowed to marry the girl whose foot fitted the shoe.

Of course, Cinderella's sisters' feet were far too big. The stepmother was trying to make the horrible pair cut off their toes when the prince spotted Cinders in her rags and called her over. As soon as she put on the shoe the prince recognised her, and they were married the next day.

They lived happily ever after, and Cinders was always nice to her sisters.

(Although some say she married them off to some really awful boys – but she wouldn't do that, would she?)

FAMOUS FAIRY TALE TELLERS

The lawyer Charles Perrault wrote many other fairy stories, including *Puss in Boots*, *Sleeping Beauty* and *Little Red Riding Hood*. He was born in Paris in 1628 and began writing stories when he was 55.

Jakob and Wilhelm Grimm also wrote many fairy tales. They were born in Kassel, Germany, in 1785 and 1786. They, too, studied law, but spent their lives collecting and retelling folk stories, including *Hansel and Gretel* and *Rapunzel*. They were known as the Brothers Grimm. Here is an extract from their tale of *Cinderella*, published in 1812. Their story was originally written in German.

> The woman had brought with her into the house two daughters, who were beautiful and fair of face, but vile and black of heart. Now began a bad time for the poor step-child. "Is the stupid goose to sit in the parlour with us?" they said. "He who wants to eat bread must earn it. Out with the kitchen-wench." They took her pretty clothes away from her, put an old grey bedgown on her, and gave her wooden shoes.

Hans Christian Andersen was born in Odense, Denmark, in 1805. He was a poor boy; his father was a shoemaker and Hans longed at first for an acting career, but failed miserably. Then, he turned his hand to story-telling and wrote 168 tales, including *The Little Mermaid*, *The Ugly Duckling*, *Thumbelina* and *The Emperor's New Clothes*. Some people say his life was a 'rags to riches' story.

The Oldest Cinderella of Them All
A tale from China

This is the oldest known Cinderella story. It comes from China during a time called the Tang dynasty, which ended more than 1000 years ago in 907 AD.

Once upon a time, a chieftain named Wu had two wives, and they lived in a cave near a river. Each woman gave birth to a girl, but soon afterwards, Chief Wu and one wife died. The little girl that had been orphaned was called Yeh-Shen, and the other wife, her stepmother, brought her up.

The stepmother spoiled her own daughter and gave Yeh-Shen the worst jobs. The only friend the girl had was a beautiful fish and, each day, she went to the river to share what little food she had with it.

One day, the stepmother went down to the river, caught the fish, killed it and cooked it.

Yeh-Shen was very upset, but an old man dressed in rags appeared and said to her,

"Don't cry. Just keep the fish bones safe, for they will grant your heart's desire."

So Yeh-Shen rescued the bones from the dung heap and hid them.

Soon it was time for the spring festival, when young people gathered in the village to find husbands and wives for themselves. Yeh-Shen longed to go, but her stepmother refused.

"My daughter must have all the attention," she said, adding spitefully, "and anyway, you're too scruffy."

Left behind in the cave, Yeh-Shen got out the fish bones.

"I wish I had some nice clothes," she said. Suddenly, she was wearing a beautiful blue dress with a cloak of kingfisher feathers. On her feet were golden slippers, whose soles were made of solid gold.

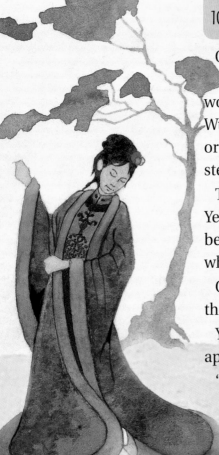

Secret magic: Yeh-Shen gets her heart's desire.

"Don't lose the slippers, Yeh-Shen," warned the fish bones. And the girl, amazed the bones could talk, stammered out a promise.

When Yeh-Shen arrived at the festival, everyone gathered around her admiringly. But she panicked when she spotted her stepmother and stepsister and ran out of the village, losing one of the slippers.

At home, she found herself once more in rags. Quickly, she got out the fish bones.

"I'm so sorry," she cried. "But I've lost one of the slippers. What shall I do?"

But the bones stayed silent, and sadly she hid the shoe she had left.

The other shoe, meanwhile, was found, and because of its beauty and obvious value, was sent as a gift to the king of T'o Han.

The king put the shoe on show in a special tent near the village where it had been found.

"Whoever it fits," he declared, "can claim it as their own."

But secretly he ordered soldiers to hide by the tent and keep watch. One dark night, Yeh-Shen slipped quietly into the tent to take the slipper; but as she turned to go the soldiers arrested her. She was taken to the king, who fell in love with her at first sight and insisted on going home with her. There she produced the other slipper and as she put them both on her feet, her rags turned back into the beautiful gown and cloak. She and the king were soon married and they lived happily ever after.

The stepmother and daughter stayed in their cave until the day they were crushed to death in a shower of flying stones.

A taste of the Tang dynasty

The Tang dynasty was a golden age for China. There were many great poets and sculptors and their society was so civilised that they even had civil service exams. The Chinese had also invented gunpowder by now and entertained themselves with fireworks – at a time when British people lived in crude houses and fought with swords and spears. It would be another 400 years before anyone in Europe had a clue about guns.

Rhodopis Steps Out for True Love

A tale from Egypt

Once upon a time, there was a young Greek girl called Rhodopis. One day, while she was out gathering seashells, pirates kidnapped her. They took her and other people they had captured to a big slave market in Egypt.

She was bought by a man who treated her kindly and took her to his house. He was a rich man, and had other slaves who were all jealous of Rhodopis' good looks. They were mean to her and made her do all the jobs they didn't like doing. But she was so sad at leaving her family that it didn't make any difference to her. Gradually, she began to feel better, and although none of the other slaves were any nicer to her, she began to make friends with the birds and animals that lived in the fields around her new home.

One day, while she was out in the fields, she met a falcon, and it flew round her head as she danced. Her master saw her dancing and was so impressed that he gave her a pair of red shoes.

When she came back to the house with the shoes, the other slaves were even more jealous and poor Rhodopis was given even more work to do. The next day, the master took his whole household to Memphis to see the Pharaoh, but Rhodopis stayed at home to grind the grain.

After Rhodopis waved them goodbye, she sat down with her shoes in her lap and thought sadly of all the bad things that had happened to her. But at that moment, the falcon, who was really the god Horus, swooped down, took one of her slippers and flew away with it.

In Memphis, the Pharaoh was sitting on his throne feeling distinctly bored, and very lonely. Everybody was always wanting him to marry, but he never found anybody he liked very much. In the middle of a feast, the falcon flew over the Pharaoh and dropped Rhodopis' slipper in his lap. Something about the shoe – perhaps one of Rhodopis' tears – made him sit up and think. He told all his servants to go out and search for the owner of the shoe. The only person the shoe would fit was Rhodopis. The other slaves were absolutely furious, and Rhodopis' master was very sad, but she was taken to the Pharaoh and they fell in love at first sight. The Pharaoh married her and they lived happily ever after.

◆ There really was a pharaoh who married a slave girl. He was called Amasis.

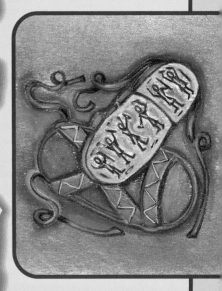

◆ Shoes in those times were simple sandals. The pharaoh Tutankhamen had a pair of sandals which showed Egypt's enemies – so that he could stamp on them while he walked!

◆ Men and women didn't dance together in ancient Egypt. Rhodopis must have been very athletic and graceful because many steps included acrobatics.

◆ Horus was the son of Osiris, the god of the underworld, and Isis, the queen of heaven and earth.

Chinye's Good Manners Pay Off
A tale from Nigeria

This is a story from Nigeria, in West Africa.

Once upon a time, there was a man who had two wives. One was beautiful and gentle and the other was evil and spiteful.

The beautiful wife had a daughter called Chinye. The evil one had a daughter called Adanma.

One day, the beautiful wife died and the evil one had to look after Chinye from then on. Chinye was as good and as beautiful as her mother and Adanma was as ugly and as spiteful as hers.

The evil stepmother wanted to get rid of Chinye, so she sent her out every night into the forest to fetch water. She hoped, you see, that Chinye would be eaten by a lion and never come back. But Chinye was so beautiful that the animals fell in love with her. The antelope and the hyena helped her to find good, fresh water and always saw her safely home.

One day, Chinye met an old woman in the forest and offered to carry a heavy cooking pot for her. The old woman was so grateful that she showed Chinye a pile of gourds and told her to pick the smallest.

When Chinye took the gourd home she broke it open, and a beautiful house sprang up around her, filled with valuable and useful things. The evil stepmother was so jealous that she sent Adanma into the forest, hoping for the same result.

When Adanma met the old woman she, too, carried the cooking pot, but only because she had been told she had to, and she was rude to the old woman. When she was shown the pile of gourds she didn't listen to the old woman's advice, and took the biggest one. But when she got it home and her mother smashed it open, a great whirlwind sprang up and destroyed their pots, pans, clothes and cowrie shells. They lost everything. They were too proud to ask Chinye for help and left the village for ever.

But Chinye used all her new-found wealth to help the people of her village and they lived happily ever after.

◆ Many people who live in Nigeria belong to the Yoruba tribe.

◆ Cowrie shells were once used as money all over the world, including China, and there are still people in Nigeria who can remember trading with these shells.

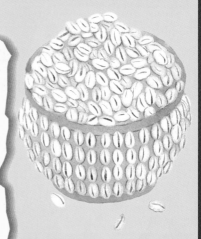

◆ Often a man in the Yoruba tribe would give a basket filled and decorated with these shells to the parents of the girl he wanted to marry.

Cindy and the Prince

By Rachel Anderson

Once upon a time, not so long ago, two moody sisters were getting ready to go to the prince's party. Alas, no amount of ribbons and bows, trinkets and tiaras, blushers and lip gloss could improve their looks.

"Haven't you ironed our dresses yet?" they screamed at their stepsister.

Cindy helped in every possible way: she crimped their hair; tightened their corsets; she varnished their nails.

She couldn't wait for them to be out of the house so she could have a bit of quiet.

"Ner ner ner!" crowed one sister. "Bet you wish you were going to the party!"

"But nah nah nah! You can't come," crowed the other. "Because *you* haven't got an invitation!"

And out the spiteful sisters flounced. They climbed into their swanky stretch limo and … two minutes later, they were back, all of a fluster.

"It won't start!" they wailed. "We're going to be late!"

Cindy asked, "When was it last serviced? Did you check the oil? Are the spark plugs clean?"

The sisters hadn't a clue. "We don't bother our pretty little heads about that kind of greasy stuff."

Cindy went out to investigate. But even she couldn't get the limo to start.

"We'll take yours," her sisters said. (Cindy had a very old banger but she kept it in tip-top running order.)

She was relieved to see them leave. She settled down by the fire with her favourite book, *Magic and the Art of Motor Maintenance.*

She was startled by a flash as her fairy godmother turned up.

"Cindy, sweetie!" trilled the FGM. "Why aren't you at the party?"

"My sisters tore up my invitation card."

With a twitch of her magic wand, the FGM magicked a replica card. With another swish, she turned Cindy's denim dungarees into cloth-of-gold hot pants and her clogs into a pair of dainty shoes.

"Cool," grinned Cindy. "But please, not glass slippers again. They're so dangerous when the heels break."

The FGM, knowing Cindy was a fitness fanatic as well as a DIY mechanic, magicked her some trainers with sparkly gold laces and platform soles. Then she did her other trick with the pumpkin, the lizards and the rats. But Cindy had no intention of riding inside a pumpkin.

"Far too sticky," she said, and she whizzed up a nourishing pumpkin soup for the FGM, the rodent footmen and lizard coachmen to enjoy.

Then, slightly reluctantly, she jogged off towards the palace.

"Don't forget to leave one of your trainers on the steps!" the FGM called after her, though Cindy had no idea why.

She passed lots of traffic queueing to get in through the palace gates and was by no means the last guest to arrive.

At the party, to her surprise, she had a wonderful time. She danced the salsa and the samba, also the rumba and the mambo. The prince, though not much of a dancer himself, thought she was amazing.

But the stepsisters were as angry as cats. "How ever did *you* learn to dance like that?" they hissed.

"Evening classes on Thursdays," smiled Cindy. "You really should come along."

Cindy didn't stay late, for she knew that an hour's sleep before midnight is always worth two after. However, she did remember to leave one trainer behind.

Next day, the prince had that tired 'morning-after-the-party' feeling until he spotted Cindy's abandoned trainer sparkling in the sunshine. He set out with a convoy of coaches filled with his courtiers in search of the trendy dancing girl. Eventually, the procession arrived at the house of the three sisters.

And whose foot did the dazzling trainer fit?

"I knew it had to be her!" screamed one of the sulky sisters. "She has all the luck."

With a courtier's help, the prince got down on one knee and proposed. "Please, would you do me the honour of becoming my wife?"

"Not flipping likely," said Cindy. "I'm not ready to settle down yet. Besides, I don't like the way you make your servants drive you about. Why can't you use your legs? You'd need to be more environmentally aware for me."

"Dear Miss," implored the prince. "I don't even know your name. But I'll do anything for you, even try and alter my ways, for I want to be with you for the rest of my life!"

"Very well, I'll think about your offer. But not right now, because first I've got to fix my sisters' ridiculous limo. And after that, there's my daily run in the park."

"However," Cindy went on, "if you were prepared to join me on my jog round the park, you never know, I might say yes. Bye for now."

"OK!" said the prince eagerly.

"See you later then. Midday, by the lake. Don't forget to bring your trainers!" said Cindy.

Here's looking at you!

Not everybody agrees on what is beautiful. This is because there are no rules about beauty; it is a matter of opinion. The idea of beauty changes, depending on when, and where, you live.

Hundreds of years ago in South America, mothers hung beads on their babies' heads, to try to make them go cross-eyed, which was thought very attractive.

Queen Elizabeth I liked to cake her face with a white powder because it was thought beautiful, and she and her ladies-in-waiting also used to put belladonna in their eyes to make their pupils grow bigger. This isn't something anyone would do today because the lead in the powder, and belladonna, are both highly poisonous.

In Charles Perrault's time, women liked putting patches, just like black spots, on their cheeks. Men wore wigs then, like some lawyers do in English courts nowadays. But they also wore tights and high-heeled shoes.

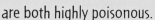

In Victorian times, it was thought important to keep as much of your body covered up as possible. Women kept their hair long and wore corsets so they could have small waists.

In some African tribes it is considered beautiful to have a long neck. Rings are used to stretch the neck.

In Europe nowadays, it's very fashionable to put rings and studs through parts of your body and to have tattoos.

In Scotland and in Tonga, in the Pacific Ocean, it is perfectly normal for men to wear skirts.

Does everyone agree what is beautiful?

Cinderella special

Are you a secret Cinderella? Do you dream of your Prince Charming? Or are you the one waving the magic wand?

Are you nice enough to be Cinders? Try our quick quiz to find out.

1 Your ugly sisters are invited to the Palace Ball and tell you that you can't go. Do you:

a do their hair for them;

b sit in your room and sulk;

c put itching powder in their underwear?

2 They leave for the ball. Do you:

a wave them goodbye with a bright smile on your face;

b have a screaming tantrum;

c pinch one of their dresses and get on your bike to the palace?

3 An old lady calls at your house when you are crying in the kitchen. Do you:

a let her in and make her a cup of tea;

b set the dogs on her;

c tell her to come back tomorrow when you're feeling better?

4 You meet someone you really like at a disco. Do you:

a dance with them all night but never tell them your name;

b pin them into a corner until they promise to see you again;

c exchange phone numbers?

5 A rich, handsome prince (OK, ordinary, guy) asks to marry you after just one dance. Do you:

a say yes immediately;

b shout, "About time too";

c say you'll think about it.

Now add up your scores: if you answered mostly a, you are a true Cinderella; mostly b, are you another ugly sister? And mostly c, you are obviously a modern girl who has no time for fairy tales.

Have a ball – have it all!
We tell you how next week.

Ask Annie: magchat's own fairy godmother helps another damsel in distress

Help! I don't know what to do. I met the boy of my dreams last night at the disco and today he wants to marry me. He's very rich and handsome and everyone says he's charming. But I have my doubts. It seemed like the start of a fairy tale romance when our eyes met across a crowded room. We danced together all night. You should have seen the look on my ugly stepsisters' faces.

I was under strict instructions to leave at midnight (my stepmum would freak if I was late), but my prince didn't want me to go.

I was in such a rush when I left, that I lost my shoe and he picked it up. Today he came round and asked me to meet his parents. When I told him I had to go to my evening class because I want to be a nuclear physicist, he just laughed and said I needn't worry my pretty little head about that sort of thing any more.

What do I do?

'Cinders',
Barons Court

STAR LETTER!

FGM says

Cinders – quit stressing. Get to know him first. If he's really keen, he'll wait. If he is your Prince Charming, he'll know you're worth waiting for. Remember, it's your life, so don't let anyone else write the ending for you – and if he's not for you, check out next week's magchat, where we'll have tons of tips for making dreams come true!

Sporting life of princes

The men that the Cinderella characters end up with are nearly always described as handsome and charming. But it goes without saying that they were also expected to be brave and good at sports.

In Charles Perrault's time, Prince Charming would be able to ride a horse and fight with a sword.

Yeh-Shen's Chinese king would have been expert at hunting with falcons and archery. He would have known how to play backgammon, which is still played today. Noblemen at that time even played polo and a kind of football.

If the Nigerian girl Chinye married, she would be looking for a warrior who was skilled at killing wild beasts with a spear.

In ancient Egypt, a prince would hunt geese by throwing sticks at them – after his trained cat had startled them from the papyrus reeds. Men also went after hippos and crocodiles with spears.

All the princes in the stories were heroes of their time. If you wrote a Cinderella story for today, what would your prince be like? Would he be sporty – a fantastic footballer, or would you rather make him clever – a computer genius? Perhaps he would be be a famous film star?

And, most important of all in a Cinderella story, would he be rich and handsome?

Alien Travel Agency

1 If warm, wet and wobbly's what you want, we've got it!

2 Boing Boing – Gateway to the Great Tortoise Park.

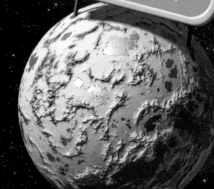

1 Barfaminits live here!

Inhabitants: The Barfaminits – webbed toes and fingers, scaly bodies, dorsal fins, gills

Favourite foods: Sea slugs and jellyfish eaten raw with plenty of salt

Climate: Humid, mainly cloudy with plenty of rain

Capital city: Deepledeepest. 70 m below sea level

Planet's surface: 2% land, 98% sea

Average water temperature: 25°C

2 Kanga-bangas r us!

Inhabitants: The Kanga-bangas – enormous feet, short arms with razor-sharp claws, enormous ears, extendable eyes on stalks, mouths like vacuum cleaners

Favourite food: Tortoises

Climate: Hot, dry; days and nights equal in length

Capital city: Shellsarus – made entirely of tortoise shells

Planet's surface: 80% land – long stretches of sandy desert, rocky hills, flat plains of grass, few trees

Average air temperature: 40°C

3 Tads' territory!

Inhabitants: The Tads – slimy, damp, green skin, warts, wide flat feet, huge mouths, large, round, staring eyes, nostrils all the way down their spines

Favourite foods: The Tarpaeain snotfly, small fish, most insects, snails

Climate: Warm, damp, frequent showers and sunny intervals

Capital city: Slugalug. 3 m above sea level

Planet's surface: 30% land, 70% open ponds, shallow lakes and small streams

Average air temperature: 24°C

WHY NOT TRY EARTH? IT'S OUT OF THIS WORLD! IT'S OUT OF THIS WORLD! IT'

3 Sad Tads? No way! Share a snotfly – see why!

5 Come alive – drive!

4 Where the fungis and fungals hang out!

6 Sssssssh! Live the quiet life.

4 The Dirty Dungarneez

Inhabitants: The Dirty Dungarneez – six legs, no noses, no eyes, long feelers, no teeth, slobbery, slimy mouths, can spit poison 50 m

Favourite foods: Rotting vegetation, mould, fungi

Climate: Foggy, drizzle, sun rarely shines

Capital city: None – at night the whole population of the Dungarneez cling together for warmth and to regurgitate food for each other to suck up

Planet's surface: 75% land mainly covered by small deciduous trees; 25% sea.

Average air temperature: 22°C

5 Yeaaangs!!!!!!!

Inhabitants: The Yeaaangs – exist only as heads wired into complex rocket-powered, eight-wheeled vehicles

Favourite food: Drive-in pizzas

Climate: Kept artificially warm and dry (so the Yeaaangs can always keep their sunroofs open), light breezes to blow away the exhaust fumes

Capital city: Motorhome. 10 m above sea level – although the thousands of multi-storey car parks rise several hundred metres into the sky.

Planet's surface: Tarmac

Average air temperature: 25°C

6 Ssssh! Murmuroids at work

Inhabitants: The Murmuroids – thin clouds of light grey gas that spread to fill available spaces.

Favourite food: None

Climate: The Murmuroids live entirely underground in total darkness; a gentle breeze moves them through the rocky tunnels that lead to …

Capital city: Big Cave

Planet's surface: Constantly bombarded by frozen asteroids

Average (underground) air temperature: 2°C

yyy.alientravelagency.arg.x*

Need a change? Tired of the same old views?

Well, why not swap your planet of birth for Planet Earth?!!

Eat cooked food!
Absorb the Sun's rays!!
Run for a bus!!!
Try on clothes!!!!
Have a haircut!!!!!
EARTH – it's out of this world!

PLANET EARTH – there's something here for everyalien.

FACT Earth has more salt-water oceans than land

FACT Earth has more species of tortoise than anywhere else in the universe

FACT Earth has deserts, grassy plains, leafy forests, rivers, lakes, ponds, streams, caves, rain, sun, mist, fog ... not to mention millions of miles of roads!

FACT Earthlings waste more food than any other creatures in the universe

FACT There's no speed limit for flying saucers!

EARTH – no one there knows you're here!

EARTH

funny place? funny people!!

Have a laugh – visit Earth:

- elegant
- easy
- enormous
- enjoy

The Alien Travel Agency challenge

You set us the challenge:

"Find ONE holiday location where EVERYALIEN can have fun."

We asked the experts.
They said it couldn't be done.

"You must be off your tiny legs!"
SPLART FAGGEENRD
(STUNK TV: THE TOP TEN DANK AND DIRTY HOLIDAY SPOTS)

"Show me – and I'll buy the rocket fuel!"
BRAIN NO. 1289456
(ZERAAAANG FREE DVD DISTRIBUTION CORPORATION: ISSUE 12654B)

We proved them wrong.

HOW?

We found Planet Earth.

Click here to download your free brochure now –
or simply call in at THE ALIEN TRAVEL AGENCY for a free mind-transfer.
(Free saucer park and ride at AlphaBeta III)

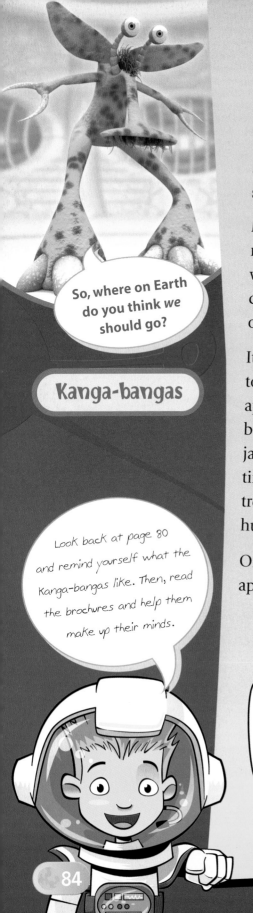

So, where on Earth do you think we should go?

Kanga-bangas

Look back at page 80 and remind yourself what the Kanga-bangas like. Then, read the brochures and help them make up their minds.

The rainforest – Brazil

The rainforest – a rip-roaring, radical roller-coaster ride of really incredible opposites! Pouring with rain one minute – bright sunshine the next – rainforests are the sunniest and the wettest places on Earth.

Massively tall trees make a warm, sunny world above and a dark, damp one below on the forest floor.

It's home to opposites too – giant eagles, great apes, huge snakes and big cats, like the deadly jaguar, live alongside tiny termites, miniature tree frogs and delicate hummingbirds.

Only a visit to the rainforest can make you truly appreciate its beauty.

Visit a rainforest while you still can. Those foolish Earthlings are cutting them down.

The Galapagos Islands – the Pacific Ocean

The Galapagos – home to creatures found nowhere else in the entire universe!!

Q: Such as?

A: How about the giant tortoise?

Q: What's so special about them?

A: Age: up to 150 years! Shells: up to 150 cm from tip to tail! Weight: over 200 kg!

Q: What else?

A: The world's only sea-going, deep-diving underwater lizard! The amazing marine iguana doesn't only swim, it can dive down to over 10 m deep and can spend up to 10 minutes underwater.

Q: Anything else?

A: How about the blue-footed booby? With its huge wingspan, this giant bird spends most of its life gliding over the waves far out at sea. It only comes to land once a year, to nest. It's so unused to walking, it spends a lot of time falling over!

Q: Sounds great. Any others I shouldn't miss?

A: Penguins, sea lions, oh, and the sea cucumber.

Q: What on earth is that?!

A: You'll just have to come and see for yourself.

The Galapagos – the only holiday animal lovers will ever want.

So, where on Earth do you think we should go?

Barfaminits

Look back at page 80 and remind yourself what the Barfaminits like. Then, read the brochures and help them make up their minds.

The Great Barrier Reef – Australia

The Great Barrier Reef – the greatest underwater experience on Earth.

Why?
Easy:

- the amazing, stupendous banks of beautiful, colourful coral;
- the incredible marine life;
- the warm, clear water – a perfect place for underwater exploration.

Did you know the Great Barrier Reef is the only thing on Earth made up of living creatures that can be seen from outer space? Not surprising as it's over 2000 km long!

the deadly lionfish

As well as the beautiful corals, the Reef is home to some other extraordinary creatures, like elegant Irukandji jellyfish, the deadly lionfish, playful bottlenose dolphins, mighty humpback whales and six species of sea turtles.

And on the Great Barrier Reef the water's always clear, inviting and warm – averaging around 25°C – it's a perfect place for diving; and the perfect place to choose for that perfect holiday.

Top of the World – the Himalayas, Nepal

Stand on the top of Mount Everest and you've really reached the heights of holiday fun!

You've reached the highest place on Earth. At 8848 m above sea level, you are standing higher than many of the aeroplanes that fly the world!

But that's not all!

The Himalayas have more than 10 other mountain peaks that tower over 7300 m!

Their very names – Annapurna, Kanchenjunga – sound like the names of heroes from the myths and legends of the past.

A Himalayan holiday is all about finding the hero inside you!

The air is thin, the air is freezing, the climbing is tough, really tough.

Are you brave enough to take up the challenge?

Can you beat the snowfields, the treacherous icy rock, the avalanches – can you beat the fear inside you and make it to the very Top of the World?

The Himalayas – only for heroes.

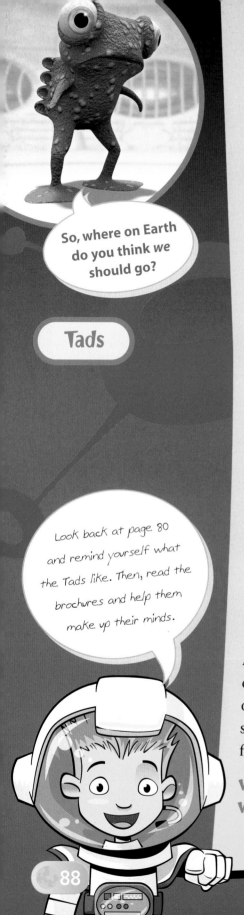

So, where on Earth do you think we should go?

Tads

Look back at page 80 and remind yourself what the Tads like. Then, read the brochures and help them make up their minds.

The Everglades – Florida, USA

The Everglades – step into one of the most unusual wetlands anywhere on Earth.

But, hey! Watch out for Ali G. Ator. Show him your toes and he'll be snacking later! Oh, oh! Alligator! These reptiles can grow up to 5 m long!

The Everglades – different from anywhere else you'll find on Earth.

As you zoom down towards the Everglades, your first thought is: 'Where's the water?' What seems to be beneath you is a great wide sunny plain of grass, waving in the warm breeze. It's only as you try to find a dry spot to land that you realise the grass is actually growing out of a great river of slow-moving fresh water creeping slowly down to the sea.

As well as being a great place to splash about in, another reason to visit the Everglades is that it is home to hundreds of fascinating creatures.

Apple snails – about the size of an egg – are everywhere. Fish? They're everywhere. And look out for our long-legged birds – herons, egrets, storks and ibises – wading through the water to find their prey.

Warm, wet and full of watery food. The Everglades. What more could you want?

The Autobahn – Germany

Some people have asked us: "A holiday on a road? You must be joking!"

But the Autobahns are no ordinary roads – they're one of the last places left on this crowded planet where keen motorists can put that accelerator down hard and DRRRRRRRRRRRRRRRIVE!

Germany – a road network second only in size to the USA. That's a lot of tarmac. Over 10,000 km and, in some places, you can drive as fast as you like!

So, take advantage of our Rent-a-FAST-car service. What do you fancy? Ferrari or Porsche? The Autobahn is just made for speed. Three lanes, and the left-hand one is just for overtaking.

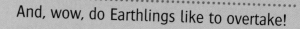

And, wow, do Earthlings like to overtake!

Don't be surprised to see your speedo needle touching 150 kph as you race down the middle lane, and then to catch a glimpse of a pair of dazzling headlights as something blurs past in the lane outside you!

You like life in the fast lane, so the Autobahn's the place to be.

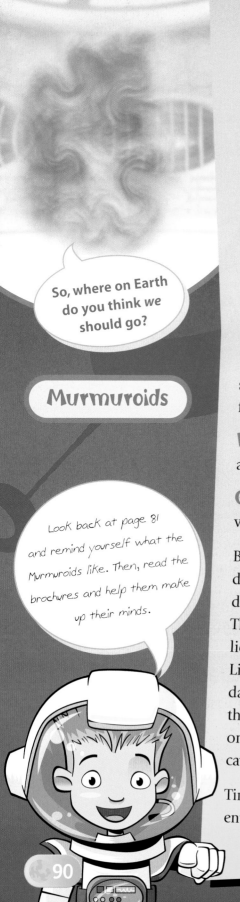

So, where on Earth do you think we should go?

Murmuroids

Look back at page 81 and remind yourself what the Murmuroids like. Then, read the brochures and help them make up their minds.

Mammoth Cave National Park – Kentucky, USA

Leave the sun behind and wander, instead, deep, deep below Earth's surface, down, down, down, through the longest caves in the world!

Now's your chance – if you take up our once-in-a-lifetime offer to visit the Mammoth Cave National Park.

Hear – the distant murmur of underground rivers echo around you as you peer down into the Bottomless Pit where no Earthling has ever stood.

Thrill – to those strangely shaped stalactites and stalagmites that leap out at you in the gleam of your flickering torch.

Be dazzled – by the walls full of glittering crystals and jewels.

Gasp – at the ghostly columns of towering rock vanishing into the shadows way, way above.

Brave enough to descend to the deepest depths of the caves? Then other surprises lie in wait for you. Living in the total darkness are some of the strangest creatures on Earth: blindfish, cave beetles and eyeless crayfish and shrimps.

Tired of the bustle of everyday life? Don't delay – enter the silent, mysterious world of Mammoth Cave.

The Sahara Desert – Africa

If you choose just one holiday this year, it must be the Sahara Experience.

Around 3.5 million square miles to explore! Endless 'seas' of sand – the famous Sahara 'ergs' – await you.

Book yourself a place on one of our dune buggy safaris and enjoy the greatest off-road adventure of your life.

For a more leisurely holiday experience, choose the traditional camel train. Travel slowly by day on your personal 'ship of the desert', camp at night under the stars and relax as our cooks prepare traditional desert meals – coffee, dates and sheeps' eyes a speciality!

Bask in the hot days, chill out in the cool nights.

The Sahara – the warmest welcome awaits you.

Postcards from Earth

All the aliens, from all six planets, chose to visit Earth for their holidays. As you can see from their postcards, they really enjoyed their holidays on Earth. But can you tell who went where? Which postcard was written by the Barfaminits, the Yeaaangs, the Tads, the Kanga-bangas, the Murmuroids, and where did the Dirty Dungarneez end up?

Yes!! They really are that big! I know!! Huge or what?? Only thing was, the crazy Earthlings don't eat them!! Uh?! You can't hunt them!! Boring, or what? But it was OK because they had this other food, called 'burgers'. They were really cool, you just roll them down the hill and chase after them. What else? Oh yes, went swimming with lizards and compared feet with the boobies. Looking forward to our first meal when we get back!!

I hope this postcard arrives quietly. We should be drifting back soon, though it will be hard to leave here. As you can see from the image on the front of this primitive communication device, we really did get away from it all. The darkness was superb, though we found the temperatures of 10°C rather hot and hard to get used to. There were other visitors, but we managed to float away from most of them, and the fish couldn't see us at all! Perfect.

Wow! You just have to come here!! We spent the whole week just going faaaast!! Four wheels and petrol power took a bit of getting used to (and so did something called 'sausages' — they outnumber pizzas about five to one), but by the end we were kings of the left-hand lane. We're bringing a thing they call 'headlights' back. Flash or what!! See you at the multi-storey.

Bit of a problem Day 1 – found ourselves on the wrong trip! Instead of warm, damp, sunny days paddling in low-lying water, we found we were going up and up and freezing the warts off our backs! But sorted it out and have just spent the week snacking on snails and splashing about. Bit of a shock when we sat down on what we thought was a log, and it opened its mouth and swallowed Granny!

Nice. Water temperature just right, salt tastes good, clear too – you can see where you're headed underwater. Great colours. Bringing back some bright red fish to brighten up the front garden. Found it a bit sunny compared to home, but the food was just great, especially the jellyfish. Yum. Missing the rain though. We waved to you. Did you see us?

Took us some time to get far enough in, but once we felt our way past the fires and the bulldozers, we found some really good places to stay. Fantastic fungi — really tasty — though you have to check first for the poisonous frogs. Great beds — rotting wood and leaves a metre deep! A bit too hot some of the time, but it rains a lot so that cools you down. The trees are immense! Make ours feel like weeds. Thought we'd try and sneak some seeds back in through customs. Looking forward to a good wet bed.

Index